THE MIRROR DEVOTIONAL

Written By: JaLisa A. Jones
Cover Design: Anais Gallop, Esteem Studios - @esteem.studios
Photography: Angelique Winfield - @bacreative
Book Design & Editing: Aaron C. Butler

© 2025 JaLisa A. Jones

ISBN 9798991412186 (Paperback)
ISBN 9798991412193 (eBook)

Library of Congress Control Number: 2025900955

All rights reserved. This book or any portion thereof may not be reproduced in any form without permission from the copyright holder, except as permitted by U.S. copyright law.

Printed in the United States of America
BookButler Publishing Company

Upper Marlboro, MD 20774

TheBookButler.com

BookButler Publishing Company titles may be purchased in bulk for educational, business, fundraising, or sales promotional use. For information, please email: info@thebookbutler.com

The Mirror Devotional

An Individual's Accountability to Healing, Transformation, and Reflecting the Identity of Christ

Written By: JaLisa A. Jones

Dedication

I dedicate my first book to the spiritual leaders who have played a profound role in shaping my life, from my youth to the present day: Pastor Leo Thorpe, Pastor Diane Mosby, and my spiritual father, Pastor Melvin O. Jiggetts. Pastor Jiggetts, thank you for continually reminding me of the greatness within and for nurturing my growth in the Word of God. A heartfelt thank you to the extraordinary women in my life who have been my sounding board, source of accountability, and prayer warriors. You know who you are! :)

Preface

James 1:23-24 (NIV): *Anyone who listens to the word but does not do what it says is like someone who looks at his face in a mirror and, after looking at himself, goes away and immediately forgets what he looks like.*

This scripture speaks to the analogy of a person looking at their reflection in a mirror to illustrate how hearing God's Word without acting on it is ineffective. Just as someone who looks in a mirror and immediately forgets their appearance, a person who hears the Word but does not apply it fails to let it transform their life. The passage emphasizes the importance of not only listening to God's Word but also living it out through obedience and action.

Jeremiah 29:13 says, *"And ye shall seek me, and find me, when ye shall search for me with all your heart."* Some of you may wonder why it feels so hard to "find" Jesus. It might seem like others have that connection, but you don't. Or maybe having a relationship with Christ feels foreign altogether. One reason for this is the condition of our hearts. Pursuing a relationship with God requires giving Him our whole heart—not fragmented pieces. I often use the analogy, we have to invite God into our entire home, not just the one room that looks good.

If taken seriously, this devotional will help reveal the condition of our hearts. It will challenge us to recognize and reflect on where our hearts truly stand. More importantly, it invites us to be honest with God about those areas. This devotional is a reminder that, without Jesus Christ, we are broken and incapable of reflecting who He has called us to be. As you seek a deeper relationship with God, be prepared to let go of your false sense of security. Know this: your vulnerability is safe with the Father.

Vulnerability is for those who value uncomfortable shedding over comfortable cycles.

Introduction
-Let's Start Here!

A few years ago, during a conversation with a friend, we often reflected on the concept, *"we don't walk around with mirrors."* That simple idea profoundly impacted me and became one of my favorite revelations. It highlights how we often fail to recognize how we present ourselves in life—whether in relationships, friendships, parenting, work, ministry, or other roles. Imagine if we carried a mirror that reflected every conversation, glance, mood, or negative posture. Have you ever considered what that reflection might reveal? On the other hand, it would also show how a smile, kindness, or welcoming posture can brighten someone's day. Regardless of the reflection, one thing is clear: mirrors have the potential to shape how we show up in the world.

A mirror's purpose is simple—to reflect whatever stands before it. Yet, as we dive deeper into this devotional, the word *mirror* takes on a more profound meaning. Beyond reflecting our physical appearance, it symbolizes self-awareness and inner truth. Could this be why reading the Bible feels like looking into a spiritual mirror? While it doesn't reflect our outward image, it reveals the state of our hearts and aligns us with the likeness of Christ.

While a physical mirror shows us what is on the surface, the spiritual mirror—the Word of God—reminds us there's so much more beneath: emotions, values, beliefs, and experiences that define who we are. Facing these inner realities requires courage and vulnerability. Many of us avoid this self-reflection because of fear, discomfort with our imperfections, or an unwillingness to confront our truths.

True growth begins when we "clean" our mirrors—both literally and spiritually. Literally, because some of us leave physical mirrors smudged and only look at the cleanest, smallest section to see a fragmented version of ourselves. Spiritually, many of us do the same. We skim over certain scriptures, avoiding the ones that challenge us to confront what's really in our hearts. But just like a dirty mirror distorts our reflection, avoiding self-examination distorts who we are meant to be.

The Holy Bible acts as our ultimate spiritual mirror. As 2 Timothy 3:16-17 (NIV) says, *"All Scripture is God-breathed and is useful for teaching, rebuking, correcting and training in righteousness, so that the servant of God may be thoroughly equipped for every good work."* This verse reminds us that scripture is not just for comfort—it's for correction and growth. My church often recites, *"We are getting better with the help of the Holy Spirit."* To truly transform, we must allow the Word of God to reflect both the things we cannot see and the things we don't want to see.

By clearing away denial and avoidance, we allow Jesus to show us who we are, whose we are, and what must change. Reading the Bible is not about finding ourselves—it's about finding Jesus. Yet, as we learn more about Him, we gain a clearer understanding of ourselves and begin to see ourselves the way Christ does. This clarity directly impacts how we live and share the gospel. To spread God's Word effectively, we must commit to healing, growing, and walking in our Christ-given identity, rather than being shaped by the pain of our past.

Do you not know that you are victorious? That you are the apple of God's eye? That He loves you so much He sent His only Son for you? You are precious in His sight. He wants you to walk in freedom, peace, and wholeness—not in fear, bondage, or brokenness.

God's desire for us is wholeness—in spirit, soul, and body. Paul confirms this in 1 Thessalonians 5:23 (KJV): *"And the very God of peace sanctify you wholly; and I pray God your whole spirit and soul and body be preserved blameless unto the coming of our Lord Jesus Christ."* Our soul—the seat of our mind, will, emotions, and imagination—often bears the weight of life's traumas and cares. If we aren't careful, those experiences can shape us into a version of ourselves that God never intended.

While physical mirrors reflect our outward appearance, the Bible reflects the condition of our hearts. Looking into this spiritual mirror can be challenging, but it's essential for genuine transformation. Avoidance of the Word often signals a deeper reluctance to face personal truths, pride, or a lack of spiritual discipline. But over the next 15 days, let us commit to this journey together. Let's meditate on God's Word, allowing Jesus to meet us where we are. May He bring healing, growth, and the clarity of identity you need to walk boldly in your purpose to fulfill the Great Commission.

You are called. You are loved. You are His. Now, let's begin the journey.

Table Of Content

Day 1: A New Beginning 1

Day 2: Reflecting Anger 5

Day 3: Reflecting Guilt & Shame 11

Day 4: Reflecting Pride 15

Day 5: Reflecting Offense 19

    Selah – take time to pause and reflect. 23

Day 6: Reflecting Grief 25

Day 7: Reflecting Unforgiveness 29

Day 8: Reflecting Gossip 33

Day 9: Reflecting Isolation 37

Day 10: Reflecting Fear 41

    Selah – take time to pause and reflect. 45

Day 11: Reflecting 'His Image' 47

Day 12: Reflecting "Let Them" 51

Day 13: Reflecting "Your Bloodline" 55

Day 14: Reflecting Rest 59

Day 15: Reflecting 'Christ and Making Disciples' 63

Conclusion 68

Day 1:

A New Beginning

___

A new beginning doesn't start with the calendar turning to January, the beginning of the week, or even the creation of a well-organized vision board. True transformation begins when we adopt a new mindset. As the saying goes, "Change your mind, and your body will follow." This principle aligns with God's Word, reminding us that lasting change happens when we allow Him to renew our thoughts.

Pastor Bettye Lyles once introduced this idea in a powerful teaching, and I've also seen it reflected in the therapeutic approach of Cognitive Behavioral Therapy (CBT). This model illustrates how our thoughts, feelings, and behaviors are interconnected, forming a triangle where each side influences the others. This truth mirrors the way God has designed us: our inward thoughts shape our outward actions.

But here's the challenge: it's hard to embrace a new mindset when we're clinging to the old one. You may have heard the saying, "If it ain't broke, don't fix it." Yet sometimes, God allows something to break in order to show us it's time for something new. A broken season, relationship, or expectation may be His way of preparing us for transformation.

When God begins something new, it may feel confusing or even uncomfortable, especially if we lack an understanding of His purpose. But remember this: God is not a God of chaos—He is a

God of order and intention. His plans for you are good, even when they challenge you to let go of the familiar.

Today, I encourage you to open your heart and mind to the new beginning God has for you. Whether it's a fresh start in your family, friendships, job, ministry, or spiritual journey, God is ready to work. Let Him guide you as you step into this new season with faith and courage.

Isaiah 43:18&19 (NIV): Forget the former things; do not dwell on the past. See, I am doing a new thing! Now it springs up; do you not perceive it? I am making a way in the wilderness and streams in the wasteland.

- ➢ What is God trying to reveal that you keep fighting?
- ➢ In what ways can you recognize God "springing up" provision or new opportunities?
- ➢ Are you wrestling because it's not how you thought it would look?

Romans 12:2 (NIV): Do not conform to the pattern of this world, but be transformed by the renewing of your mind. Then you will be able to test and approve what God's will is—his good, pleasing and perfect will.

- ➢ God what patterns are you trying to break in my life to become more like Christ?
- ➢ Reveal to me the areas that need to be transformed to embrace my new beginning?
- ➢ How will this new beginning reflect God's glory?

Don't Do It Without God:

Take time to sit with the Holy Spirit, by inviting God into your space and reflecting on these questions. Ask Holy Spirit to provide the same anointing and boldness Jesus had when He walked the Earth to bring change. Pray not your will be done, but your will aligns with the purpose and plan God has for your life. In Jesus name, Amen.

Prayer:

      Heavenly Father, thank You for being the God of new beginnings. Help me to release the old mindsets and habits that no longer serve Your purpose in my life. Renew my mind and align my thoughts with Your truth. I trust You to lead me into this new season, knowing that Your plans are good. May this transformation bring You glory. In Jesus name, Amen.

JaLisa A. Jones

Day 2:

Reflecting Anger

Have you ever stopped to ask yourself, "Why am I so angry?" Often, we don't take the time to dig deep and examine the root of our anger. Instead, we may find it easier to wear anger like armor, a false sense of protection. Complete transparency, I too, have been guilty of this behavior. Anger can feel empowering—making us believe we're justified or dominant—but in reality, it often reveals deeper emotions like fear, sadness, or disappointment.

The truth is, anger is a secondary emotion. Beneath it lies hurt, unmet expectations, or unhealed wounds. While anger itself is not sinful, it becomes dangerous when we allow it to control our decisions and actions. We should never allow anger to operate in the driving seat of our lives. Left unchecked, anger can destroy relationships, opportunities, and even our blessings from God. Never allow a temporary emotion, to lead to permanent outcomes we cannot change.

Jesus provides the perfect example of how to manage anger in a way that honors God. When He overturned the tables in the temple, His anger was righteous—it came from a place of love for God's house and people. He didn't allow anger to consume Him or lead Him to sin. His actions were controlled, purposeful, and rooted in truth *(Matthew 21:12-13)*.

How often do we let our anger dictate our choices instead of surrendering it to God? The Bible reminds us not to let anger take root in our hearts. We must guard against making anger an idol, something we rely on to feel strong or in control. Instead, we are called to trust God with our emotions and allow Him to transform us through His Spirit.

Here are four steps to begin surrendering your anger to God:

1. **Admit that you struggle with anger.** Honesty is the first step to healing.
2. **Recognize control issues.** Often, anger arises when we feel powerless. Trust in God's sovereignty instead of your ability to control outcomes.
3. **Acknowledge the pain beneath your anger.** Ask God to heal the wounds and disappointments hidden in your heart.
4. **Trust God with your anger.** He can handle your emotions and guide you toward peace.

When we allow the Holy Spirit to work in our hearts, He teaches us to respond with wisdom and grace. These steps are wise and practical. They reflect a journey of humility, introspection, and faith. Inviting the Holy Spirit to transform our hearts is key to breaking free from the chains of anger and replacing it with the fruits of the Spirit: love, joy, peace, patience, kindness, and self-control *(Galatians 5:22-23)*.

Psalms 37:8 (NIV): *Refrain from anger and turn from wrath; do not fret-it leads only to evil.*

Ephesians 4:26 (NIV): *"In your anger do not sin": Do not let the sun go down while you are still angry.*

James 1:19 (NLT): *Understand this, my dear brothers and sisters: You must all be quick to listen, slow to speak, and slow to get angry.*

Today, take some time to reflect on how you manage anger.

Ask God for the strength to surrender it to Him and grow in spiritual maturity.

What consequences resulted from your anger?

How do you plan to walk in victory over anger?

Break the Cycle:

1. Recognize the Triggers

Identify the situations, people, or circumstances that consistently provoke anger. Pay attention to patterns—what tends to set you off? Journaling or reflecting on these moments can help you pinpoint the root cause, which is often deeper than the immediate situation.

2. Pause Before Reacting

When anger arises, pause before responding. This gives you time to process your emotions rather than acting impulsively. Try This: Count to ten, take deep breaths, or step away from the situation momentarily. These small pauses help diffuse heightened emotions.

3. Challenge Your Thoughts

Anger often stems from assumptions, misinterpretations, or exaggerated thoughts. Ask yourself: Am I seeing this clearly?

Or is my reaction proportionate to the situation? Replace anger-fueling thoughts with more rational ones.

4. Express Yourself Constructively

Instead of suppressing or exploding with anger, learn to express it in healthy ways. Use "I" statements to communicate feelings (e.g., "I feel upset when this happens because…"). Focus on resolving the issue rather than assigning blame.

5. Practice Empathy

Try to see the situation from the other person's perspective. Understanding their feelings or motives can soften your emotional response.

6. Develop Healthy Outlets

Find ways to release built-up tension or stress that might fuel anger. Exercise, journaling, prayer, or creative hobbies can help process emotions. Practice relaxation techniques like deep breathing, meditation, or progressive muscle relaxation.

7. Seek Resolution, Not Revenge

Anger often escalates when you focus on retaliation or proving a point. Shift your focus to finding solutions and fostering peace.

8. Forgive and Let Go

Holding on to resentment keeps you stuck in the anger cycle. Forgiveness doesn't excuse the offense but frees you from its control.

9. Set Boundaries

If certain people or situations repeatedly provoke anger, set healthy boundaries to protect your emotional well-being.

10. Seek Help if Needed

If anger feels uncontrollable or affects your relationships and well-being, seek guidance from a trusted counselor, pastor, or therapist.

Breaking the cycle of anger isn't about eliminating it entirely—it's about learning to manage it in a way that honors God, fosters healthy relationships, and promotes personal peace. As Ephesians 4:26 reminds us: "In your anger, do not sin." With God's help and intentional practice, you can replace destructive anger with patience, understanding, and self-control.

Don't Do It Without God:

Take time to sit with the Holy Spirit, by inviting God into your space and reflecting on these questions. Ask Holy Spirit to provide the same anointing and boldness Jesus had when He walked the Earth to bring change. Pray not your will be done, but your will aligns with the purpose and plan God has for your life. In Jesus name, Amen.

Prayer:

Lord, I come to You with my heart wide open. I admit that anger has sometimes ruled my thoughts and actions. Forgive me for the times I have allowed it to hurt others or dishonor You. Help me to dig deeper and uncover the pain or fear behind my anger. Transform my heart through Your Holy Spirit so that I can walk in love, peace, and self-control. Teach me to trust You with my emotions and my circumstances. In Jesus name, Amen.

Day 3:

Reflecting Guilt & Shame

_____

Guilt and shame—emotions we all encounter—are often seen as twins, working together to weigh us down. Guilt whispers, "Look at what you've done," while shame shouts, "You are what you've done." Both can serve a purpose in leading us to repentance and growth, but when left unchecked, they become chains that bind us, pulling us away from God's love and purpose for our lives.

Have you been walking under the heavy burden of guilt or shame? Do you feel stuck in a cycle of self-punishment, believing the lie that your mistakes define you? I've been there too. For so long, I carried the weight of my past, thinking it was my responsibility to bear. But the truth is, we were never meant to carry such a load.

God, in His infinite love, sent Jesus to break those chains. Jesus bore our guilt and shame on the cross so we could walk in freedom. When we cling to these destructive emotions, we deny the full power of His sacrifice. It's as if we're saying, "What You did wasn't enough." But friend, it is enough.

Guilt and shame can distort how we see ourselves, keeping us from looking in the mirror and seeing the beauty of God's creation. They can also keep us from opening the Word of God, convincing us we are unworthy of His love. But today, hear this:

God loves you deeply, not because of what you've done, but because of who He is.

It's time to lay the weights down. The burden of guilt and shame is too heavy for you to carry, but Jesus is ready to take it from you. He is calling you to step into His freedom, to embrace His forgiveness, and to walk boldly in your purpose.

Isaiah 61:7 (NIV): *Instead of your shame you will receive a double portion, and instead of disgrace you will rejoice in your inheritance. And so you will inherit a double portion in your land, and everlasting joy will be yours.*

John 8:36 (NIV): *So if the Son sets you free, you will be free indeed.*

Hebrews 10:22 (NIV): *let us draw near to God with a sincere heart and with the full assurance that faith brings, having our hearts sprinkled to cleanse us from a guilty conscience*

- ➤ In what ways have guilt and shame held you back in life?
- ➤ How has guilt and shame tried to alter who God called you to be?
- ➤ Will you decide today to trust God with your guilt and shame?
- ➤ See yourself free and rejoice! (Listen to song No Bondage by Jubilee Worship)

Don't Do It Without God:

Take time to sit with the Holy Spirit, by inviting God into your space and reflecting on these questions. Ask Holy Spirit to provide the same anointing and boldness Jesus had when He walked the Earth to bring change. Pray not your will be done, but your will aligns with the purpose and plan God has for your life. In Jesus name, Amen.

Prayer:

Heavenly Father, thank You for Your endless love and forgiveness. I come to You today, laying down the guilt and shame I've carried for far too long. Help me to embrace the freedom You have given me through Jesus. Teach me to walk in confidence, knowing that I am not defined by my past but by Your grace. In Jesus name, Amen.

JaLisa A. Jones

Day 4:

Reflecting Pride

___

Pride is not limited to thinking too highly of ourselves; it also includes thinking too lowly of ourselves. Both extremes of pride can deceive us, leading to rebellion against God. The Bible speaks of the many forms of pride and the destruction it can cause. Pride blinds our spiritual vision, painting a glossy layer of deception that convinces us we know better than God. False humility, where we belittle ourselves, is a subtle form of pride. It can lead to disobedience, which ultimately results in rebellion against God. Instead of humbling ourselves and addressing the areas where we fall short, pride tempts us to focus only on the small "clean" spots in the mirror of our hearts.

Jeremiah 17:9 reminds us that the heart is deceitful and desperately wicked, full of selfish motives. Pride can manifest as feeling "not good enough" or "unworthy" to evoke sympathy or avoid responsibility. It can also show up as arrogance, presumption, or insolence, making us enemies of God. Pride prioritizes being right, winning, and seeking validation over walking humbly in truth. Jesus demonstrates how He rebuked pride, by walking in a Godly humility and serving others.

This can be a difficult truth to confront, as many of us may not recognize pride in our own hearts. But today, take a moment to pray and ask God to reveal how pride has taken root in your life. Pride hinders our effectiveness in God's Kingdom, blocks healing, and damages relationships. It thrives in isolation and rejects accountability. Pride seeks adoration for the flesh. But its path always leads to a fall.

Today, declare: "I come out of agreement with pride." Ask God to expose any areas where pride has taken precedence over His truth. As you humble yourself before Him, you will find freedom, healing, and restoration. Only a surrendered heart can truly glorify God and walk in the fullness of His purpose.

Proverbs 16:18 (KJV): *Pride goeth before destruction, And an haughty spirit before a fall*

1 John 2:26 (KJV): *For all that is in the world, the lust of the flesh, and the lust of the eyes, and the pride of life, is not of the Father, but is of the world.*

- Do you struggle with pride?
- In what ways have you wanted to be right, instead of righteous?
- Who have you offended because of pride?
- How do you think pride has led to rebellion against God?
- Identify someone who will hold you accountable in moments you may be operating in pride.

Don't Do It Without God:

Take time to sit with the Holy Spirit, by inviting God into your space and reflecting on these questions. Ask Holy Spirit to provide the same anointing and boldness Jesus had when He walked the Earth to bring change. Pray not your will be done, but your will aligns with the purpose and plan God has for your life. In Jesus name, Amen.

Prayer:

Lord, I humbly come before You, asking You to search my heart and reveal any areas of pride. Help me to reject both arrogance and false humility, and instead walk in true humility that honors You. I surrender my motives, my thoughts, and my actions to You. Teach me to trust Your Word above all else and to live in obedience to Your will. In Jesus name, Amen.

JaLisa A. Jones

Day 5:

Reflecting Offense

_____

Pastor Craig Groeschel once said, "Being offended is inevitable, but living offended is a choice." As believers, this truth challenges us to examine how we respond when we feel hurt or disrespected. The Cambridge Dictionary defines offense as an act of upsetting or insulting someone through words or actions. While offense will come, the danger lies in allowing it to take root in our hearts.

When we adapt to the spirit of offense, it can manifest as resentment, irritability, or intrusive thoughts. Have you ever caught yourself assuming others are talking about you or feeling the need to prove yourself? Sometimes, we even hold onto offense, hoping to make others feel the pain we've endured. But this cycle of hurt and bitterness keeps us stuck—unable to love like God, glorifying self over Him, and trapped in a victim mindset.

One of the roots of offense is insecurity, often stemming from a deep wound left by someone we trusted. When unresolved, that wound grows, taking over our hearts. Scripture reminds us, though, that whatever we feed will grow (Galatians 6:7-8). If we nourish offense, it will dominate our lives. But if we feed our spirit with God's love and truth, we can overcome it.

Here are practical ways to defeat the spirit of offense:

1. **Seek Godly wisdom**—Turn to Scripture and wise counsel for guidance *(James 1:5)*.

2. **Lead with love**—Respond to others with grace and patience *(1 Corinthians 13:4-7)*.

3. **Lower your expectations**—Remember that people are human and flawed, just like you *(Psalm 103:14)*.

4. **Increase appreciation for God's grace**—Reflect on how much you've been forgiven *(Ephesians 2:8)*.

5. **Forgive and let go quickly**—Don't allow offense to fester *(Ephesians 4:31-32)*.

6. **Pray for the offender and yourself**—Intercede for healing and a softened heart (Matthew 5:44).

7. **Ask God for forgiveness**—Confess how you may have offended Him daily *(1 John 1:9)*.

These steps require humility and help us confront our own imperfections. They don't dismiss the offense but allow us to release its hold on us. When we break free from the spirit of offense, we protect our hearts from becoming hardened and draw closer to God.

Don't Do It Without God:

Take time to sit with the Holy Spirit, by inviting God into your space and reflecting on these questions. Ask Holy Spirit to provide the same anointing and boldness Jesus had when He walked the Earth to bring change. Pray not your will be done, but your will aligns with the purpose and plan God has for your life. In Jesus name, Amen.

Prayer:

Father today, I petition you to search my heart. God if there is any area where offense has taken root, I ask that you pluck up right now, in the name of Jesus. God I surrender offense to you, trusting that your grace is sufficient to heal and restore. God please forgive me, for how I have offended others, intentionally or unintentionally. Most importantly forgive me for offending you. God thank you for the revelation, forgiveness is not about excusing the wrong but about freeing your heart to live in the fullness of God's love. Thank you Jesus for demonstrating how to deal with offense. In Jesus name, Amen.

Selah

Take time to pause and reflect.

If you've made it to Day 5, I'm so proud of you. You've chosen to pursue Jesus Christ and invite Him into the hidden places of your soul.

If you've completed each daily prompt so far, you're putting in the effort, and I couldn't be more proud of your dedication.

Take a moment now to pause and rest in the stillness of God's presence. Allow yourself to become comfortable simply being with Him. I believe God is proud of the work you're doing, too.

After you've rested, do something that brings you joy! We'll continue this journey tomorrow—only 10 days to go! You're uncovering a new and beautiful version of yourself by simply learning the ways of Christ and allowing His ways to transform you.

JaLisa A. Jones

Day 6:

Reflecting Grief

_____

Before we begin, I want to acknowledge that grief is a deeply personal and necessary process. This devotion is not meant to minimize the weight of grief, but to help us examine how we process it in the light of God's truth.

Grief is a natural response to loss. The National Hospice and Palliative Care Organization defines it as "the normal and natural response to the loss of someone or something important to you." In therapy, the cycles of grief are often described as denial, anger, bargaining, depression, and acceptance. Yet grief isn't limited to death. We grieve the loss of jobs, relationships, dreams, and even places. These losses are tied to our souls because they were part of us—they shaped our routines, memories, and expectations.

Grief, at its core, is evidence of love. But when that love or attachment is severed, our hearts ache for something to fill the void. And if we're not careful, instead of running to Jesus with our pain, we run to things that can never truly satisfy. These may include excessive drinking, spending, promiscuity, or overworking—what therapists call maladaptive behaviors.

What have you run to in your grief?

God has shown me that when we don't surrender our grief to Him, unhealthy spiritual patterns can form, such as:

1. **Unforgiveness** – Holding onto bitterness toward others or even toward God.
2. **Idolatry** – Placing our comfort, relationships, or coping mechanisms above God.
3. **Emotional Displacement** – Misdirecting our pain onto people or situations that don't deserve it.
4. **Isolation** – Cutting ourselves off from the community of believers.
5. **Stagnation/Regression** – Becoming emotionally stuck at the point where the trauma occurred and struggling to grow beyond it; losing progress in your spiritual journey and development.

When these patterns take root, they invite spiritual warfare. The enemy thrives on keeping us stuck and distracted in our pain, far from the healing presence of God.

But here's the hope: grief doesn't have to define us. God promises that for those who love Him, joy comes in the morning. Mourning is not the end of the story. In fact, as believers in Christ, we can claim the promise that joy is found even in the *mourning.*

Lamentations 3:32-33 (NIV): *Though he brings grief, he will show compassion, so great is his unfailing love. For he does not willingly bring affliction or grief to anyone.*

Psalms 34:18 (NIV): *The Lord is close to the brokenhearted and saves those who are crushed in spirit*

Matthew 5:4 (KJV): *Blessed are they that mourn: for they shall be comforted*

1 Thessalonians 4:13-14 (NIV): *Brothers and sisters we do not want you to be uninformed about those who sleep in death, so*

that you do not grieve like the rest of mankind, who have no hope. For we believe that Jesus died and rose again, and so we believe that God will bring with Jesus those who have fallen asleep in him.

- ➢ Take a moment to reflect. What have you been grieving?
- ➢ Have you allowed that grief to draw you closer to Jesus, or have you been running to something else to cope? The key to finding joy in the mourning is surrendering your grief to Him.

Break the Cycle:

This week, take one step toward healing. Whether it's spending time in prayer, reaching out to a trusted friend, or diving into God's Word, invite Jesus into your grief. He's waiting to carry you through it and lead you to joy.

Don't Do It Without God:

Take time to sit with the Holy Spirit, by inviting God into your space and reflecting on these questions. Ask Holy Spirit to provide the same anointing and boldness Jesus had when He walked the Earth to bring change. Pray not your will be done, but your will aligns with the purpose and plan God has for your life. In Jesus name, Amen.

Prayer:

Lord, I come to You with my pain and loss, knowing You understand my grief. Teach me to lay my burdens at Your feet and trust You to fill the void in my heart. Help me resist the distractions and lies of the enemy, and lead me into Your promise of joy that comes in the morning. Thank You for Your healing presence and unfailing love. In Jesus name, Amen.

JaLisa A. Jones

Day 7:

Reflecting Unforgiveness

When I think about unforgiveness, the phrase "sink or swim" comes to mind. While it's often used in a different context, it's striking how holding onto unforgiveness can cause us to sink. Remember the wise words of "Prophet" Dory from *Finding Nemo*: "Just keep swimming." On a deeper level, harboring unforgiveness prevents us from moving forward, dragging us down into bitterness.

The world often tells us it's okay to hold grudges or boast about refusing to forgive, but what good does it do? Holding onto unforgiveness is like drinking poison and expecting someone else to suffer. The truth is, it only harms us.

Many of us struggle with forgiveness because it feels like giving up control. We think that holding onto the offense gives us power or ensures justice. Sometimes, we fear forgiveness means excusing the offense or letting the other person off the hook. Other times, we've become so comfortable in the role of the victim that it feels like part of our identity.

But unforgiveness changes us—and not for the better. When unforgiveness takes root, it hardens our hearts. Over time, it seeps into every aspect of our lives, causing us to hurt others who had nothing to do with our pain. It robs us of peace and joy, leaving us miserable and unable to pinpoint the source of our unhappiness.

The Bible teaches us about the power of forgiveness. Jesus modeled forgiveness, even toward Peter, who denied Him, and Judas, who betrayed Him. And in *Matthew 6:14-15*, we're reminded that forgiving others is not optional—it's essential for receiving God's forgiveness.

I know forgiveness can feel impossible, especially when the hurt runs deep. You may be thinking, "You don't know what they did to me." But here's the hard truth: holding onto that pain isn't helping you. It's time to stop carrying the burden and give it to God.

God didn't design us to carry the weight of unforgiveness. It's toxic, and over time, it changes who we are. But God, in His mercy, can carry what we cannot. When we forgive, we reflect the love of Christ, who forgives us daily despite our own shortcomings.

Break the Cycle:

Think about how often we hurt God—choosing sin over Him, forgetting Him when life is good, and calling on Him only when we're in trouble. Yet, He forgives us every time. He welcomes us with open arms, provides for us, and never withholds His love.

Oprah Winfrey once said, "Forgiveness is giving up the hope that the past could be any different." I say, "as believers, we rest in a greater hope: the peace of God and the promise of new beginnings. Forgiveness is not about rewriting the past—it's about trusting God with the future."

The world says forgiveness takes time, but God says forgiveness takes faith and effort. It is a choice we make daily. The longer we hold onto unforgiveness, the harder it becomes to let go. But today, you can choose differently.

Release the burden to God, trust Him with your hurt, and allow Him to heal your heart. Forgiveness is not just about setting someone else free—it's about setting yourself free.

Matthew 6:14 (NLT): *If you forgive those who sin against you, your Heavenly Father will forgive you.*

Colossians 3:13 (NLT): *Make allowance for each other's faults and forgive anyone who offends you. Remember, the Lord forgave you, so you must forgive others*

Ezekiel 36: 26 (KJV): *A new heart also will I give you, and a new spirit will I put within you: and I will take away the stony heart out of your flesh, and will give you an heart of flesh.*

- ➢ Is there someone you need to forgive today? Ask God for the strength to release that burden.
- ➢ What steps can you take to cultivate a heart of forgiveness in your daily life?

Don't Do It Without God:

Take time to sit with the Holy Spirit, by inviting God into your space and reflecting on these questions. Ask Holy Spirit to provide the same anointing and boldness Jesus had when He walked the Earth to bring change. Pray not your will be done, but your will aligns with the purpose and plan God has for your life. In Jesus name, Amen.

Prayer:

Heavenly Father, thank You for Your endless mercy and grace. Help me to forgive as You have forgiven me. Teach me to release the burden of unforgiveness and rest in Your peace. Heal my heart, soften it with Your love, and guide me to reflect Your forgiveness in all I do. In Jesus name, Amen.

JaLisa A. Jones

Day 8:

Reflecting Gossip

_____

Gossip is a subtle but destructive force in our lives. It has become so normalized in our culture that it often goes unnoticed as a behavior that needs to change. Yet, gossip has the power to destroy friendships, families, ministries, and opportunities. When we gossip, we are essentially saying, "I have the right to speak negatively or ignorantly about someone else." This mindset is rooted in entitlement, which is closely tied to pride.

Day by day, we must confront this truth: gossip doesn't just harm others; it damages our relationship with God and reveals deeper issues within ourselves. Many of us gossip because it temporarily boosts our self-esteem or distracts us from our own struggles. Instead of fixing our eyes on God's purpose for our lives, we become "marketing agents" for the problems of others.

Another damaging aspect of gossip is its ability to create counterfeit intimacy. Relationships built on gossip are not genuine. They are fragile, shallow connections that fall apart over time. Have you ever noticed how some people default to gossip as soon as they engage in conversation? Or how others might grow frustrated with you when you refuse to participate in gossip? These moments are opportunities for us to reflect on the foundation of our relationships. Are our conversations centered on God, personal growth, and encouragement? Or are they dominated by idle chatter about others?

Instead of gossiping, consider these alternatives:

- Pray for the person being discussed.
- Seek ways to offer help and support.
- Take the matter to God, asking for wisdom and discernment.
- Use the moment to reflect on your own life and heart.

The truth is, gossip reflects a lack of purpose and focus. As sons and daughters of the Most High, we are called to live with intention and to offer hope, love, and wisdom to others. Gossip has no place in a life surrendered to Christ. As *Proverbs 13:14* or *1 Peter 5:3* reminds us, we are meant to mentor and encourage one another—not tear each other down but be examples.

When gossip arises, let it be a reminder of how much we need Jesus. Scripture warns us about the damage gossip can do. Proverbs 16:28 says, "A perverse person stirs up conflict, and gossip separates close friends." Even Jesus shut down unproductive conversations. When one of His disciples asked about another's path, Jesus replied, *"What is that to you? You must follow Me" (John 21:22)*.

Today, let's choose to walk in the newness of who we are in Christ. Gossip is not part of the kingdom life we are called to live. Let us speak words that build up, heal, and encourage. Ask the Lord to guard your heart and lips, and let's commit to being a light in our words and actions.

Leviticus 19:16 (NIV): *"Do not go about spreading slander among your people."* '*Do not do anything that endangers your neighbor's life. I am the Lord.*

Proverbs 17:4 (NIV): *A wicked person listens to deceitful lips; a liar pays attention to a destructive tongue*

Proverbs 20:19 (NIV): *A gossip betrays a confidence; so avoid anyone who talks too much*

Proverbs 26:20 (NIV): *Without wood a fire goes out; without a gossip a quarrel dies down*

Ephesians 4:29 (KJV): *Let no corrupt communication proceed out of your mouth, but that which is good to the use of edifying, that it may minister grace unto the hearers.*

- ➢ Are your conversations more focused on others' faults than on God, personal growth, or encouragement?
- ➢ What steps can you take today to replace gossip with prayer, support, or self-reflection?
- ➢ Be accountable; what damage have you caused concerning others with your mouth?
- ➢ Ask God for forgiveness and turn away from gossip.

Don't Do It Without God:

Take time to sit with the Holy Spirit, by inviting God into your space and reflecting on these questions. Ask Holy Spirit to provide the same anointing and boldness Jesus had when He walked the Earth to bring change. Pray not your will be done, but your will aligns with the purpose and plan God has for your life. In Jesus name, Amen.

Prayer:

Lord, search my heart and reveal any area where gossip has taken root. Help me to honor You with my words and relationships. Teach me to speak life and truth, and remind me of the power of my words. Guide me to focus on You and the purpose You have called me to. In Jesus name, Amen.

JaLisa A. Jones

Day 9:

Reflecting Isolation

_____

Today, let's dive right in: **Isolation is not your promise!**

There's a growing trend, especially on social media, where people proudly declare, "I'm just going to be on my own." But here's the truth—nothing about isolation is healthy. Many of us experienced forced isolation during the pandemic, and we saw firsthand how damaging it could be. Let me remind you: **God did not create you to live in isolation.**

We often try to justify isolation by saying it's how we grow, but this idea is a lie straight from the enemy. The truth is, **God does not isolate—He separates.** And there's a notable difference. Separation will occur when those relationships threaten your well-being, God's calling on your life, or shift in a season. However, when God separates, He will replace.

In the Garden of Eden, when God created Adam, He said, "It is not good for man to be alone" (Genesis 2:18). From the beginning, we were created for connection and relationship. Isolation, on the other hand, is something used in prisons as punishment or in psychiatric units during crises. It leaves people alone, unsupported, and cut off. But separation—God's way—is different. When God separates us, He's shifting our environment or relationships for a purpose. It may be uncomfortable, but it doesn't mean we're alone or without His help.

Some of us have even experienced **unconscious isolation**—when we're physically around others but emotionally withdrawn. We may say, "I don't deal with people like that," but deep down, it's often a trauma response. Fear, hurt, and disappointment have caused us to draw inward and refuse to trust. This isn't God's design; it's a trap set by the enemy to keep us from the blessings of relationship and community.

Have discernment and guard your heart, but don't isolate yourself. Why? Because isolation has serious consequences. Studies show it can lead to depression, anxiety, poor sleep, and even cognitive decline. Spiritually, isolation is the devil's playground. When we're alone, the enemy attacks our minds with lies and ungodly thoughts. But when we're part of a godly community, we don't have to fight those battles alone.

I'll be honest—there are times when I don't feel strong enough to pray for myself. In those moments, my trusted circle steps in, encouraging me, standing in agreement with me for breakthroughs, and helping me rest when I'm overwhelmed. **This is the power of godly community.**

The Bible is filled with reminders of the importance of unity, harmony, and supporting one another. We can't say we love God but hate or avoid our neighbors. Relationships are powerful because they reflect truths about ourselves that we can't see alone. When someone says, "I don't deal with people," what they're often saying is, "I can't deal with myself."

Think about the people Jesus dealt with—people with all kinds of issues, backgrounds, and beliefs. Yet, He didn't isolate Himself. Instead, He relied on the Holy Spirit to guide His interactions. Even when He sent the disciples out, He sent them in pairs (Mark 6:7). As a minister, therapist, and child of God, I've learned to use Jesus' example of engaging with others as my blueprint to reflect His nature and purity. I also rely on the Holy

Spirit to cultivate the fruit of the Spirit in me, overcoming my fleshly nature.

So today, let's resist the temptation to isolate. Let's invite God into our relationships, allow the Holy Spirit to guide us, and embrace the connections He has placed in our lives.

Genesis 2:18 (TPT): *Then Yahweh-God said, "It is not good for the man to be alone. Therefore, I will fashion a suitable partner to be his help and strength."*

Ecclesiastes 4:9-12 (NIV): *⁹ Two are better than one, because they have a good return for their labor: ¹⁰ If either of them falls down, one can help the other up. But pity anyone who falls and has no one to help them up. ¹¹ Also, if two lie down together, they will keep warm. But how can one keep warm alone? ¹² Though one may be overpowered, two can defend themselves. A cord of three strands is not quickly broken.*

Acts 2:42-47 (NIV): *⁴² They devoted themselves to the apostles' teaching and to fellowship, to the breaking of bread and to prayer. ⁴³ Everyone was filled with awe at the many wonders and signs performed by the apostles. ⁴⁴ All the believers were together and had everything in common. ⁴⁵ They sold property and possessions to give to anyone who had need. ⁴⁶ Every day they continued to meet together in the temple courts. They broke bread in their homes and ate together with glad and sincere hearts, ⁴⁷ praising God and enjoying the favor of all the people. And the Lord added to their number daily those who were being saved.*

1 Thessalonians 5:11 (NIV): *Therefore encourage one another and build each other up, just as in fact you are doing.*

- ➢ Have you been avoiding cultivating godly relationships?
- ➢ Reflect on your reasons for isolating; do you think that's God's best for you?

➢ Remember Day 7; who do you need to forgive?

Don't Do It Without God:

Take time to sit with the Holy Spirit, by inviting God into your space and reflecting on these questions. Ask Holy Spirit to provide the same anointing and boldness Jesus had when He walked the Earth to bring change. Pray not your will be done, but your will aligns with the purpose and plan God has for your life. In Jesus name, Amen.

Prayer:

Lord, thank You for creating us to live in relationship with You and others. Help me to resist the lie of isolation and embrace the gift of community. Heal any wounds or fears that keep me from trusting others. Surround me with people who will encourage, uplift, and sharpen me. Teach me to reflect Your love in my relationships and remind me that I don't have to walk this journey alone. In Jesus name, Amen.

Day 10:

Reflecting Fear

_____

We've all heard the saying "faith over fear." It's a powerful phrase, but it often sparks different interpretations. Today, let's seek clarity through the guidance of the Holy Spirit. To start, it's important to distinguish between fear as an emotion and fear as a spirit.

The emotion of fear is normal and serves a purpose—it alerts us to potential danger, whether it's a threatening situation, a painful experience, or even something as simple as a scary movie. In a healthy context, this emotion is temporary. You feel it, process it, and move forward.

However, the spirit of fear is entirely different. It doesn't come from God. As 2 Timothy 1:7 reminds us: "For God has not given us a spirit of fear, but of power and of love and of a sound mind" (NKJV). The spirit of fear is from the enemy, designed to paralyze your faith and lead you into disobedience. When fear dominates your soul, it hinders your ability to walk in God's will, replacing faith with doubt and leaving you vulnerable to destruction.

Key: The enemy is ALWAYS after your faith.

So, if God doesn't give us a spirit of fear, what does He give? Power, love, and a sound mind. These are your spiritual tools to overcome fear. To evaluate whether you are operating in faith or fear, ask yourself:

1. Are you walking in the authority of who God called you to be, or do you shrink back in doubt?
2. Have you stepped out in faith to pursue the vision God has placed in your heart—whether it's starting a ministry, a business, or a new endeavor?
3. Do you lead with love and self-discipline, or are you overwhelmed by indecision and racing thoughts?

Now, let's look at faith. Hebrews 11:1 defines it this way: "Now faith is the substance of things hoped for, the evidence of things not seen" (KJV). In simple terms, faith is not a feeling—it's a choice. Fear causes you to wallow, but faith propels you to walk forward.

Faith requires seeing with your spiritual eyes, not your physical ones. Faith allows you to envision the family restored, the business thriving, the healing manifesting, and the breakthrough coming—even when the circumstances seem bleak. This is what it means to walk by faith and not by sight (2 Corinthians 5:7).

Remember, faith is how we please God. Without it, we rely on our own strength, which inevitably leads to burnout, anxiety, and, yes, fear. But when we apply faith—real, unwavering trust in God—we tap into His power. We experience His peace and align ourselves with His perfect will.

If you want to see transformation in your life, start with faith. Surrender your fears to God and choose to trust Him with the unseen. With faith, you're no longer relying on your own strength, but on His infinite power.

Today, choose faith over fear. Walk in the power, love, and sound mind that God has freely given you. Trust Him to guide your steps, and watch how He turns your faith into victory.

Challenge: The scriptures are not listed for today's devotional. I want to challenge you to conduct a study on faith. Pick up your Bible or utilize the Bible app and search the scriptures, how God's people demonstrated great faith. Here's a few names to help you get started; Abraham, Peter, Moses, David, Esther, Deborah, or Martha.

Don't Do It Without God:

Take time to sit with the Holy Spirit, by inviting God into your space and reflecting on these questions. Ask Holy Spirit to provide the same anointing and boldness Jesus had when He walked the Earth to bring change. Pray not your will be done, but your will aligns with the purpose and plan God has for your life. In Jesus name, Amen.

Prayer:

Heavenly Father,

Thank You for being the source of all strength, peace, and love. I come to You today, humbly asking for an increase in my faith. Help me to trust You wholeheartedly, even when I can't see the way forward. Teach me to walk by faith and not by sight, and remind me that You are always working for my good, even in the unseen.

Lord, when fear tries to creep into my heart, replace it with Your perfect peace. Strengthen my spirit so I may boldly walk in the power, love, and sound mind You have given me. Help me to surrender my doubts and anxieties to You, trusting that You hold every detail of my life in Your hands.

Father, grow my faith so that I may please You in all that I do. Let my steps be guided by Your Word, my decisions rooted in Your wisdom, and my heart fixed on Your promises. May I see with eyes of faith, envisioning the plans You have for me, plans to prosper me and not to harm me, plans to give me hope and a future.

Thank You, Lord, for being faithful even when I falter. I trust in Your unfailing love and ask for Your strength to remain steadfast in every season. May my life reflect the fullness of faith in You, bringing glory to Your name.

In Jesus mighty name, I pray,

Amen.

Selah

Take time to pause and reflect.
_____

If you've made it to Day 10, it means you've taken the step to clean the mirror—picking up the Word of God and allowing Him to reveal your true identity. You've chosen to see yourself as God created you to be, not what the world has tried to shape you into.

Day 10 signifies that you're growing in your knowledge of Jesus Christ. As you reflect His nature, you're drawing closer to the person God has called you to become. Remember, this journey isn't about achieving perfection but embracing steady progress.

I pray you've been thoughtfully answering the questions and digging deep into your reflections. Always keep in mind: God can't heal what you choose to hide.

You're uncovering a renewed and refreshed version of yourself simply by learning Christ's ways and allowing His truth to transform your life.

The next five days will be about walking boldly in the new life God has for you!

For today, find rest in the stillness of God. Put away distractions and simply rest. Your ability to rest, is a direct reflection of your ability to trust God.

JaLisa A. Jones

Day 11:

Reflecting 'His Image'

In today's world, so much revolves around image. Social media platforms bombard us with curated lives and filtered moments, pushing us to focus on how we appear to others. From trends and styles to belief systems and body ideals, we often allow these fleeting standards to shape our identity. But here's the question we must ask ourselves:

Why look to creations, instead of the Creator for your identity?

The world's identities are ever-changing, but God's design for us is eternal. Platforms like Instagram, Snapchat, or TikTok may entertain or inspire us, but they don't define who we truly are. Our worth, value, and purpose are found in the One who made us, not in the approval or validation of others.

James 1:23-25 provides a powerful reminder:

"Do not merely listen to the word, and so deceive yourselves. Do what it says. Anyone who listens to the word but does not do what it says is like someone who looks at his face in a mirror and, after looking at himself, goes away and immediately forgets what he looks like. But whoever looks intently into the perfect law that gives freedom and continues in it—not forgetting what they have heard, but doing it—they will be blessed in what they do."

When we allow social media or others to dictate our identity, we are like the person who forgets their reflection in the mirror. Instead, God calls us to look intently into His Word, where our true reflection is found.

Stop seeking validation from people who can't validate themselves.

The world encourages us to pursue popularity, but God calls us to pursue intimacy with Him. The question isn't, "Does the world know me?" but rather, "Does Jesus know me?"

When we reflect God's image, we embody the characteristics of Christ. Anger, pride, gossip, and unforgiveness begin to fade, replaced by peace, humility, love, and grace. A light shines through us—a light that the world cannot ignore.

The enemy wants you to believe that following Christ means giving up too much, but the truth is that surrendering to Him leads to freedom. Living apart from God may seem fun, but it often leaves us feeling empty and bound. In Christ, we gain everything—peace, joy, purpose, and a confidence rooted in faith.

- Who do you want to reflect: the world or Christ?
- Can you accept that you are made in God's image?
- Are there aspects of your life that go against who God has called you to be?

Break the Cycle: Ask God to help you see yourself as He sees you. Let go of what the world says about you and embrace the freedom of being His child. Spend time meditating on scriptures that affirm your identity in Christ. Here are a few to start:

Genesis 1:27 (KJV): *So God created man in his own image, in the image of God created he him; male and female created he them.*

2 Corinthians 5:17 (KJV): *Therefore if any man be in Christ, he is a new creature: old things are passed away; behold, all things are become new.*

Psalm 139:14(KJV): *I will praise thee; for I am fearfully and wonderfully made: marvellous are thy works; and that my soul knoweth right well.*

Ephesians 2:10 (KJV): *For we are his workmanship, created in Christ Jesus unto good works, which God hath before ordained that we should walk in them.*

1 Peter 2:9 (KJV): *But ye are a chosen generation, a royal priesthood, an holy nation, a peculiar people; that ye should shew forth the praises of him who hath called you out of darkness into his marvellous light;*

Galatians 2:20 (KJV): *I am crucified with Christ: nevertheless I live; yet not I, but Christ liveth in me: and the life which I now live in the flesh I live by the faith of the Son of God, who loved me, and gave himself for me.*

Galatians 2:20 (TPT): *My old identity has been co-crucified with Christ and no longer lives. And now the essence of this new life is no longer mine, for the Anointed One lives his life through me—we live in union as one! My new life is empowered by the faith of the Son of God who loves me so much that he gave himself for me, dispensing his life into mine!*

Don't Do It Without God:

Take time to sit with the Holy Spirit, by inviting God into your space and reflecting on these questions. Ask Holy Spirit to provide the same anointing and boldness Jesus had when He walked the Earth to bring change. Pray not your will be done, but your will aligns with the purpose and plan God has for your life. In Jesus name, Amen.

Prayer:

I will not be providing a prayer on today's devotional. If you have not done so already, I want to give God your heart in prayer. God wants to hear directly from you. Today, write down you're the prayer on your heart.

Day 12:

Reflecting "Let Them"

___

As a therapist, one of the foundational principles I guide my clients through is understanding that we are not in control of others—nor can we control how they feel or think about us. Pastor Melvin O. Jiggetts wisely said, "How others feel or think about you, is not your business."

As your life begins to transform, not everyone will be happy for you. At first, they may celebrate your change, but when it starts to inconvenience them or limit their access to you, challenges can arise. My pastor once reminded me: when people see you growing, and the evidence of God's blessing is upon your life, they may begin to treat you or respond to you differently. However, here's the key: let them.

Your job is not to fix how others feel about you; your job is to pray for them and keep walking. You are entering a season that requires full commitment and focus on Christ. To thrive in this season, you must embrace the mindset of "let them."

Until you master the power of "let them," you might feel tempted to retaliate, become passive-aggressive, or match their negative energy. But your new nature is a reflection of Christ. You are called to let your light shine, trusting that God sees everything. Romans 12:19 (NLT) reminds us: "Dear friends, never take revenge. Leave that to the righteous anger of God. For the

Scriptures say, 'I will take revenge; I will pay them back,' says the Lord."

Jesus Himself demonstrated the power of this "let them" mentality. He was misunderstood, rejected, falsely accused, and even betrayed by those closest to Him. Yet, He didn't retaliate or try to convince others of who He was. Instead, He continued to fulfill His purpose, trusting His Father to handle everything. In Matthew 26:53-54, when Peter tried to defend Him during His arrest, Jesus said, "Do you think I cannot call on my Father, and He will at once put at my disposal more than twelve legions of angels? But how then would the Scriptures be fulfilled that say it must happen in this way?"

Remember, God sees every hurt, every slight, every misunderstanding. Anyone who hurts you also hurts God's heart. Trust Him to handle it. Stop trying to play God by seeking revenge or being vindictive.

If you allow it, "let them" can become a powerful mantra in your life. By adopting this mindset, you free yourself from the burdens of others' actions and attitudes. Instead, you'll propel forward into the next level of your walk with Christ, filled with peace and purpose.

Let them doubt you.

Let them walk away.

Let them misunderstand you.

And as they do, let God handle the rest.

Ephesians 4:31-32(NIV): *³¹ Get rid of all bitterness, rage and anger, brawling and slander, along with every form of malice. ³² Be kind and compassionate to one another, forgiving each other, just as in Christ God forgave you.*

Ecclesiastes 3:6 (KJV): *A time to get, and a time to lose; a time to keep, and a time to cast away;*

Proverbs 15:1 (KJV): *A soft answer turneth away wrath: but grievous words stir up anger.*

Philippians 3:13-14 (KJV): *¹³ Brethren, I count not myself to have apprehended: but this one thing I do, forgetting those things which are behind, and reaching forth unto those things which are before, ¹⁴ I press toward the mark for the prize of the high calling of God in Christ Jesus.*

James 4:7 (NIV): *Submit yourselves, then, to God. Resist the devil, and he will flee from you.*

Proverbs 29:11(NIV): *Fools give full vent to their rage, but the wise bring calm in the end.*

- ➢ Do you believe the "let them" mentality will improve your walk with Christ?
- ➢ Do you find yourself obsessing over what others think of you?
- ➢ Have you tried to manipulate how people see you?
- ➢ How can Galatians 5:22 assist with the "let them" mentality?
- ➢ How do you perceive this ministering to others watching your walk of faith?

Don't Do It Without God:

Take time to sit with the Holy Spirit, by inviting God into your space and reflecting on these questions. Ask Holy Spirit to provide the same anointing and boldness Jesus had when He walked the Earth to bring change. Pray not your will be done, but your will aligns with the purpose and plan God has for your life. In Jesus name, Amen.

Prayer:

Lord, help me release the need to control how others think or feel about me. Teach me to trust You with every misunderstanding, rejection, or hurt. Strengthen my heart to let go of offense and embrace peace. Remind me that You see all and will handle what I cannot. Fill me with grace, patience, and focus as I walk in Your purpose. In Jesus name, Amen.

Day 13:

Reflecting "Your Bloodline"
___

As we begin today's devotional, let's approach it with open hearts and minds, free from offense and full of expectation for what God wants to do in our lives and families. Family is precious—a gift from God—and often serves as the foundation of our lives. However, even within this sacred unit, we can recognize patterns or behaviors that have been passed down for generations.

This reflection is not about judgment but about opportunity. You have the unique chance to intercede for your family, break harmful cycles, and establish a legacy rooted in Christ. Through prayer, reflection, and bold faith, you can be the change agent God calls you to be.

Take time to reflect on your family's history. Write down the generational blessings—those gifts, talents, and strengths that have been evident in your lineage. Perhaps it's creativity, academic excellence, financial stability, or athletic ability. These are gifts from God, and acknowledging them allows you to celebrate His goodness.

Next, prayerfully identify areas of struggle in your family. These generational curses might manifest as poverty, addiction, sickness, or broken relationships. As you reflect, remember that Christ has redeemed you and given you the power to overcome.

Coming into relationship with Christ means you are now part of a new family—the family of God. His blood covers and cleanses every sin, every curse, and every stronghold in your life and your bloodline. Standing boldly for Christ sometimes means standing against patterns in your family that do not align with His will.

God is clear: no idols should come before Him—not even our families. While we honor and love our families, God must remain the highest authority in our lives.

Break the Cycle:

If you've ever wondered why certain struggles persist in your family or why progress feels delayed, know this: it can stop with you. Through the power of prayer and faith in Jesus, you can be the one to break the cycle.

Here are four steps to include in your prayers for your family:

1. **Repentance:** Pray for the sins of your bloodline, both known and unknown, across generations.
2. **Renounce:** Come out of agreement with generational struggles, whether they are sicknesses, addiction, poverty, or other behavioral patterns.
3. **Replace:** Speak and declare God's promises over your family.
4. **Plead the Blood:** Cover your family and future generations with the cleansing blood of Jesus.

Exodus 20:5-6 (NIV): *⁵ You shall not bow down to them or worship them; for I, the Lord your God, am a jealous God, punishing the children for the sin of the parents to the third and fourth generation of those who hate me, ⁶ but showing love to a thousand generations of those who love me and keep my commandments.*

Numbers 14:18 (NIV): *'The Lord is slow to anger, abounding in love and forgiving sin and rebellion. Yet he does not leave the guilty unpunished; he punishes the children for the sin of the parents to the third and fourth generation.'*

Jeremiah 17:5 (NIV): *This is what the Lord says: "Cursed is the one who trusts in man, who draws strength from mere flesh and whose heart turns away from the Lord.*

Galatians 5: 1(NIV): *It is for freedom that Christ has set us free. Stand firm, then, and do not let yourselves be burdened again by a yoke of slavery.*

Matthew 16:19 (NIV): *I will give you the keys of the kingdom of heaven; whatever you bind on earth will be bound in heaven, and whatever you loose on earth will be loosed in heaven."*

James 5:16 (NIV): *Therefore confess your sins to each other and pray for each other so that you may be healed. The prayer of a righteous person is powerful and effective.*

1 John 1:9 (NIV): *If we confess our sins, he is faithful and just and will forgive us our sins and purify us from all unrighteousness.*

Don't Do It Without God:

Take time to sit with the Holy Spirit, by inviting God into your space and reflecting on these questions. Ask Holy Spirit to provide the same anointing and boldness Jesus had when He walked the Earth to bring change. Pray not your will be done, but your will aligns with the purpose and plan God has for your life. In Jesus name, Amen.

Prayer:

Heavenly Father, in the name of Jesus, I repent for my sins and the sins of my family. I lift up the generations before me and pray for Your mercy. I renounce any agreement with sickness, poverty, addiction, and other strongholds in my bloodline. I declare that these chains are broken in Jesus' name.

Father, I replace these struggles with Your promises. I speak healing, peace, abundance, and freedom over my family and future generations. Your Word says we are more than conquerors, and I declare that victory belongs to my bloodline. Lord, may Your Spirit guide us, and may the blood of Jesus wash us clean. In His powerful name, Amen.

Reflection:

Take time this week to meditate on God's promises and write down the blessings and breakthroughs you want to see in your family. Declare that the old has passed, and a new legacy in Christ has begun. Through His power, you can set a new course for generations to come.

Be encouraged: it stops with you, and it starts with Him.

Day 14:

Reflecting Rest

_____

Scripture:

"Come to me, all you who are weary and burdened, and I will give you rest. Take my yoke upon you and learn from me, for I am gentle and humble in heart, and you will find rest for your souls." – Matthew 11:28-29

In a world that celebrates hustle and constant activity, rest often feels like a forgotten treasure. Society pushes the narrative that our value is tied to productivity, but God calls us to a different rhythm—one of work balanced with rest. Rest is not a sign of laziness; it is an act of trust in God's provision and care.

God created us to need rest, and He models it for us. Even in creation, God rested on the seventh day, not because He was tired, but to establish a rhythm of rest for us (Genesis 2:2-3). Jesus also exemplified this during His ministry. Though He had an urgent mission, He took time to withdraw, pray, and rest.

When we refuse to rest, we risk more than physical exhaustion; we jeopardize our ability to hear God's voice. Rest quiets the noise of life and makes room for God's whispers to reach our hearts. It allows us to refuel, renew, and remain effective in the work of the Kingdom.

Wearing busyness like a badge of honor can quickly turn into idolizing work, placing it above our relationship with God. But when we embrace rest, we declare that our worth comes from God, not from what we accomplish.

By choosing rest, we set an example for others to do the same. As followers of Christ, let's model a lifestyle of balance that reflects the peace and trust we have in Him.

Exodus 33:14 (NIV): *"The Lord replied, "My Presence will go with you, and I will give you rest."*

Matthew 11:29 (NIV): *"Take my yoke upon you and learn from me, for I am gentle and humble in heart, and you will find rest for your souls."*

Psalms 91:1(NIV): *"Whoever dwells in the shelter of the Most High will rest in the shadow of the Almighty."*

Psalm 23:2 (KJV): *"He maketh me to lie down in green pastures: He leadeth me beside the still waters."*

Isaiah 30:15 (NIV): *"This is what the Sovereign Lord, the Holy One of Israel, says: "In repentance and rest is your salvation, in quietness and trust is your strength, but you would have none of it."*

- Do you struggle to rest?
- Do you feel guilty when attempting to rest?
- What are some ways you can engage in self-care?
- How can rest influence how you see Christ?

Don't Do It Without God:

Take time to sit with the Holy Spirit, by inviting God into your space and reflecting on these questions. Ask Holy Spirit to provide the same anointing and boldness Jesus had when He walked the Earth to bring change. Pray not your will be done, but your will aligns with the purpose and plan God has for your life. In Jesus name, Amen.

Prayer:

Heavenly Father, thank You for the gift of rest. Forgive us for the times we've neglected it, trying to do things in our own strength. Teach us to prioritize rest as a way of honoring You and caring for the bodies, minds, and spirits You've entrusted to us. Help us to hear Your voice more clearly as we embrace stillness. May our lives reflect a balance that draws others to Your peace. In Jesus name, Amen.

JaLisa A. Jones

Day 15:

Reflecting 'Christ and Making Disciples'

As we conclude this 15-day journey, let's take a moment to praise God for the strength, focus, and grace that brought us here. Completing this devotional is an accomplishment, but it doesn't have to be the end of your time in God's Word. Let this be the beginning of a deeper, daily walk with Him.

Reaching Day 15 shows you've been intentional in seeking God. My prayer is that you didn't rush through these chapters, but allowed the truth of God's Word to truly transform your heart and mind.

One of the most important takeaways from this journey is the call to make disciples. Receiving salvation is personal, but it's not the end goal—it's the starting point of a life meant to reflect Christ. Salvation is the foundation, but discipleship is where we grow into the fullness of God's plan for us. If you reflect your identity in Christ, then you naturally reflect discipleship.

In Matthew 16, Jesus teaches the cost of following Him. It requires surrender—letting go of things, people, and environments that bring us comfort outside of Him. Why? Because God wants our whole hearts, undivided by anything else. When we let other things permeate, the spaces meant for Him, we miss the fullness of His presence and purpose.

Psalm 23 reminds us of this truth: "The Lord is my Shepherd; I shall not want." This is where God desires us to be—a place of spiritual contentment, where we lack nothing because our confidence is fully rooted in Him.

Matthew 28 calls us to "go therefore and make disciples." You might wonder: How can I make disciples if I'm not a pastor or preacher? The truth is, you don't need a title to lead others to Christ. What you do need is a clear understanding of who God is, what it means to be saved, and how to live out your faith.

Here are three ways to embrace discipleship:

1. **Lead by example.** Your life is the loudest sermon you'll ever preach. People will notice Christ through your actions more than your words.
2. **Use your God-given design.** God created you with unique gifts and passions that align with His will. Discovering your purpose often comes as you grow closer to Christ. Remember, your purpose isn't always tied to your job—your job might simply be the means to support your calling.
3. **Plant seeds of faith.** Not every encounter will lead someone to salvation, but every conversation about Jesus can plant a seed. Trust God to water those seeds in His timing.

The first 10 days of this devotional focused on personal healing and preparation. Why? Because unresolved pain can hinder our ministry. Instead of leading people to Christ, we risk hurting them by ministering out of our wounds. That's why we cried out to God for healing—to show up not as perfect people, but as vessels with hearts surrendered to Christ.

Being a disciple doesn't require perfection; it requires obedience and a willingness to reflect Christ in all you do.

Break the Cycle:

Discipleship starts with intentionality. Break the cycle of fear, hesitation, or uncertainty by taking one simple step this week to share your faith or reflect Christ's love. Here are some practical ideas:

- Pray for someone in your life who needs encouragement or to know Christ.
- Invite a friend or coworker to church or a Bible study.
- Share a personal testimony of God's goodness with someone in need of hope.
- Offer to serve in a ministry or volunteer for a community outreach.
- Spend time mentoring or encouraging a younger believer in their walk with Christ.

Remember, discipleship is not about grand gestures—it's about consistency and obedience in the small moments. Trust that God will work through you as you step out in faith.

Reflection Questions:

- Do you know your God-given purpose?
- Have you been hesitant to share your faith with others? Why?
- What steps can you take to become bolder in your walk with Christ?

Let us go forward with confidence, knowing that we are chosen, equipped, and empowered to be change agents in the world. God has called us to reflect His love, share His truth, and make disciples wherever we go.

Matthew 28: 19-20 (NIV): *"Therefore go and make disciples of all nations, baptizing them in the name of the Father and of the Son and of the Holy Spirit, and teaching them to obey everything I have commanded you. And surely I am with you always, to the very end of the age."*

John 4:2 (NIV): *"although in fact it was not Jesus who baptized, but his disciples."*

Romans 8:28 (NIV): *"And we know that in all things God works for the good of those who love him, who have been called according to his purpose."*

Jeremiah 29:11 (NIV): *"For I know the plans I have for you," declares the Lord, "plans to prosper you and not to harm you, plans to give you hope and a future."*

Proverbs 19:21 (NIV): *"Many are the plans in a person's heart, but it is the Lord's purpose that prevails."*

John 14:12 (NIV): *"Verily truly I tell you, whoever believes in me will do the works I have been doing, and <u>they will do even greater things than these</u>, because I am going to the Father."*

Don't Do It Without God:

Take time to sit with the Holy Spirit, by inviting God into your space and reflecting on these questions. Ask Holy Spirit to provide the same anointing and boldness Jesus had when He walked the Earth to bring change. Pray not your will be done, but your will aligns with the purpose and plan God has for your life. In Jesus name, Amen.

Prayer:

Heavenly Father,

Thank You for the gift of life, health, and strength. Above all, thank You for Your Son, Jesus, who came to be an example and endured the cross for my sins. Lord, help me to live a life that is pleasing in Your sight and fruitful in reaching both the saved and the lost.

Fill me with Your Holy Spirit and grant me a deeper understanding of Your Word. Let my life reflect Your nature so that I may faithfully spread the gospel and make disciples for Your glory.

In Jesus name, I pray. Amen.

Conclusion

I sincerely pray that this devotional has inspired and encouraged you in your faith journey. My hope is that its impact does not stop with you but becomes a gift you share with others—whether through conversations with friends, discussions in your church groups, or moments with your family. Be creative in how you use it, even incorporating it as a resource during a fast.

I wholeheartedly believe this devotional can transform lives, and I cannot wait to hear your testimonies. Please take a moment to leave a review and share your experience.

Remember, growth in faith does not happen overnight—it's a journey of consistent progress. Take it one step at a time and celebrate getting better along the way.

If I could leave you with one last piece of encouragement, it would be this: During a critical season in my life, a woman named Freda Wilkins would often ask me, *Where do you see Jesus in that?* At first, I found it frustrating, but over time, I realized she was teaching me something invaluable—how to shift my perspective away from myself and refocus on Christ. That lesson has stayed with me, and now I pass it on to you. As you continue to grow, take a moment to ask yourself, *Where do I see Jesus in this?*

I am humbled by the calling God has placed on my life to bridge gaps and break generational curses through the lens of theology and therapy. With gratitude, I thank Him for trusting me with this assignment, and I am honored to walk this journey with you.

-Y'all be blessed, peace!

ABOUT THE AUTHOR

JaLisa A. Jones is a passionate minister, licensed professional counselor, and community leader from South Hill, Virginia, now residing in Richmond. With a deep love for helping others heal and grow as disciples, she serves as an Associate Minister at Churchland North Baptist Church in Portsmouth, Virginia, under the leadership of Pastor Melvin O. Jiggetts.

JaLisa integrates ministry and mental health counseling, guided by her belief that faith and therapy are deeply interconnected. As a Licensed Professional Counselor, she specializes in helping individuals and families break cycles, overcome challenges like anxiety, depression, and trauma, and discover their God-given potential.

In 2021, she founded the Purposeful H.E.R. Foundation, a nonprofit devoted to empowering women and girls to heal and thrive. She's also the creator and co-host of the podcast Cranberry Juice in a Wine Glass, where real-life struggles meet faith and accountability.

When she's not counseling or ministering, JaLisa is a gifted singer with a rich gospel music background, a member of Delta Sigma Theta Sorority, Incorporated, and an all-around lover of crab legs, poetry, and quality time with loved ones.

JaLisa's mission is simple yet powerful: to bridge gaps and break strongholds through the lens of theology and therapy; helping others find healing, hope, and freedom in Christ.

www.ingramcontent.com/pod-product-compliance
Lightning Source LLC
LaVergne TN
LVHW070938070526
838199LV00035B/651